Post Cards from
NATI...

∽ A Vintage Post Card Book ∽

FARCOUNTRY
PRESS
Helena, Montana

Fred Kiser served as the official Great Northern Railway photographer from 1906 to 1912. *Tomar Jacob Hileman* became the railway's official photographer in 1925. Their black-and-white photographs were colorized and used to help promote the railway's new rail line to Glacier National Park.

ISBN 10: 1-56037-394-6
ISBN 13: 978-1-56037-394-0
© 2006 Farcountry Press

Postcards are from the private collection of John Chase, Great Falls, MT.

For more information about our books:
write Farcountry Press, P.O. Box 5630, Helena, MT 59604;
call (800) 821-3874; or visit www.farcountrypress.com.

Created, produced, and designed in the United States.
Printed in China.

Glacier National Park

Mountain goat. Photo by Hileman.

Post Cards from Glacier National Park © 2006 Farcountry Press

Post Card

Two Medicine Lake and Mount Rockwell
near Two Medicine Camp,
Glacier National Park, Montana.

Glacier National Park

Two Medicine Lake and Mount
Rockwell near Two Medicine Camp.
1912. Kiser Photo Co., Great Northern Railway.

Post Cards from Glacier National Park © 2006 Farcountry Press

Post Card

Glacier National Park

Sperry Chalets. Photo by Hileman.

Post Card

Post Cards from Glacier National Park © 2006 Farcountry Press

The Blackfeet Indians use Glacier National Park as a Summer Camping Ground.

Glacier National Park

One of several postcards in a
souvenir folder sold circa 1930s.

Great Northern Railway.

Post Card

Place
Stamp
Here

5801. Forest Lobby, Glacier Park Hotel, Eastern Gateway to Glacier National Park, Montana.

Glacier National Park
Forest Lobby, Glacier Park Hotel.

Post Cards from Glacier National Park © 2006 Farcountry Press

Post Card

Glacier National Park

Lake McDonald. Photo by Hileman.

Post Cards from Glacier National Park © 2006 Farcountry Press

Post Card

Glacier National Park

Auto busses at St. Mary Chalet.

Photo by Hileman.

Post Card

Grinnell Lake and Glacier, Glacier National Park.

Glacier National Park

Grinnell Lake and Glacier. Photo by Hileman.

Post Card

Post Cards from Glacier National Park © 2006 Farcountry Press

Glacier National Park

Gunsight Lake and Mount Jackson.

Kiser Photo Co., Great Northern Railway.

Post Cards from Glacier National Park © 2006 Farcountry Press

Post Card

Glacier National Park
St. Mary Lake from St. Mary Chalet.

Photo by Fred Kiser.

Post Cards from Glacier National Park © 2006 Farcountry Press

Post Card

Glacier National Park

Bear Grass on Iceberg Lake Trail.

Photo by Hileman.

Post Cards from Glacier National Park © 2006 Farcountry Press

Post Card

Morning Eagle Falls, Glacier National Park.

Glacier National Park

Morning Eagle Falls. Photo by Hileman.

Post Cards from Glacier National Park © 2006 Farcountry Press

Post Card

Glacier National Park

Glacier Park Hotel. Photo by Hileman.

Post Card

Post Cards from Glacier National Park © 2006 Farcountry Press

Glacier National Park
Swiftcurrent Falls, Gould Mountain.
Photo by Hileman.

Post Card

Post Cards from Glacier National Park © 2006 Farcountry Press

Cut Bank Camp on Cut Bank River,
Glacier National Park.

Glacier National Park
Cut Bank Camp on Cut Bank River.
1912. Kiser Photo Co., Great Northern Railway.

Post Card

Post Cards from Glacier National Park © 2006 Farcountry Press

Glacier National Park

Heavens Peak from Granite Park
Chalets. Photo by Hileman.

Post Cards from Glacier National Park © 2006 Farcountry Press

Post Card

Glacier National Park
Lobby, Lake McDonald Hotel.
Photo by Hileman.

Post Card

Post Cards from Glacier National Park © 2006 Farcountry Press

Avalanche Lake, Nine Miles from Lake McDonald,
Glacier National Park.

Glacier National Park

Avalanche Lake, nine miles from
Lake McDonald. 1909. Kiser Photo Co.,
Great Northern Railway.

Post Card

Place
Stamp
Here

Glacier National Park

Going-to-the-Sun Road. Photo by Hileman.

Post Card

Post Cards from Glacier National Park © 2006 Farcountry Press

Glacier National Park

Little Chief Mountain from Going-to-
the-Sun Chalets. Photo by Hileman.

Post Card

Post Cards from Glacier National Park © 2006 Farcountry Press

Glacier National Park

Many Glacier Hotel. Photo by Hileman.

Post Card

Post Cards from Glacier National Park © 2006 Farcountry Press

On Trail at Base of Goat Mountain,
One Mile from Going-to-the-Sun Camp,
Glacier National Park.

5345. © 1911 BY KISER PHOTO CO., FOR GREAT NORTHERN RAILWAY

Glacier National Park

On trail at base of Goat Mountain, one mile from Going-to-the-Sun Camp.

1911. Kiser Photo Co., Great Northern Railway.

Post Cards from Glacier National Park © 2006 Farcountry Press

Post Card

Hotel at Belton, Mont. Entrance to Glacier National Park. On Line of Great Northern Railway.

Glacier National Park

Hotel at Belton, Montana, entrance
to Glacier National Park.

Post Cards from Glacier National Park © 2006 Farcountry Press

Post Card